# Bull Sharks

BY LAURA HAMILTON WAXMAN

AMICUS HIGH INTEREST • AMICUS INK

Amicus High Interest and Amicus Ink are imprints of Amicus
P.O. Box 1329, Mankato, MN 56002
www.amicuspublishing.us

Library of Congress Cataloging-in-Publication Data
Names: Waxman, Laura Hamilton, author.
Title: Bull sharks / by Laura Hamilton Waxman.
Description: Mankato, MN : Amicus High Interest, [2017] |
 Series: Sharks | Audience: K to grade 3._ | Includes index.
Identifiers: LCCN 2015033748| ISBN 9781607539766
 (library binding) | ISBN 9781681520896 (pbk.) | ISBN
 9781681510101 (ebook)
Subjects:  LCSH: Bull shark–Juvenile literature.
Classification: LCC QL638.95.C37 W39 2017 | DDC
 597.3/4–dc23
LC record available at http://lccn.loc.gov/2015033748

Editor: Wendy Dieker
Series Designer: Kathleen Petelinsek
Book Designer: Aubrey Harper
Photo Researcher: Rebecca Bernin

Printed in the United States of America.

HC 10 9 8 7 6 5 4 3 2 1
PB 10 9 8 7 6 5 4 3 2 1

# Table of Contents

# A Forceful Hunter

A hungry bull shark swims below the surface of the ocean. It is slowly trailing a tasty fish. Suddenly, it speeds up. Bam! It slams hard into the surprised fish. Then it opens its jaws and bites down with its pointy teeth. Fish for lunch! Yum!

This bull shark is looking for a good meal. Watch out, fish!

The bull shark's wide body looks like a bull. That's how it got its name.

 How big are bull sharks?

A bull shark is a medium-sized shark. But its body is wider than most sharks. That makes this shark look thick and sturdy. A bull shark has dark gray skin on top. It has white skin on the bottom. The skin is thick. It feels rough and it is tough. It protects the shark in the water.

 Bull sharks are about 11.5 feet (3.5 m) long. That's about as long as two grown people!

A bull shark has two small eyes. The eyes are on the sides of its head. It has a short, round **snout**. It has big jaws that open wide. Inside are many sharp teeth. Each tooth is shaped like a pointy saw.

A bull shark's mouth is full of sharp teeth. One bite can do lots of damage.

You have arms and legs. But sharks have fins. The fins are stiff and strong. They help a shark swim fast. A bull shark has eight fins. Two **dorsal fins** are on its back. Two **pectoral fins** stick out from its sides. It has two **pelvic fins** under its body. The **anal fin** is close to the tail fin.

A shark's strong tail fin pushes it through the water.

# Catching Dinner

Snap! A bull shark shuts its jaws. It caught a fish. Bull sharks hunt and eat other animals. They are **predators**. Bull sharks mostly hunt fish and small sharks. But they will hunt many kinds of **prey**. They eat turtles and birds. They eat shellfish, too. They even eat dead animals.

This sea turtle's shell is no match for a bull shark's strong jaw and sharp teeth.

A bull shark's head is made for hunting. It can sense the movements of prey nearby.

Bull sharks hunt in shallow coastal waters. They also hunt in large rivers that connect to the ocean. Bull sharks can sense prey moving in the water. They can also smell prey. Scientists aren't sure how well these sharks see. But bull sharks don't seem to need good eyesight to find a meal.

A bull shark hunts near the bottom of an ocean or river. When it finds its prey, it follows behind very slowly. Then it races forward with a sudden burst of speed. It slams its head into the prey. The animal is stunned. It doesn't move. That's when the shark uses its sharp teeth to eat the prey.

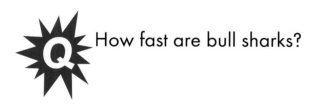 How fast are bull sharks?

**This bull shark gobbles up a fish near the ocean floor.**

 Bull sharks can swim about 11 miles per hour (18 kph).

Two bull sharks come together to make baby sharks. Babies grow inside their mother.

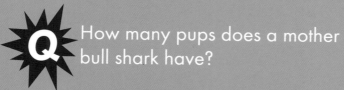

**Q** How many pups does a mother bull shark have?

# Having Babies

It's summer. The water is warm. Two
bull sharks have come together to **mate**.
Baby bull sharks begin to grow inside their
mother. They are born about a year later.
The baby sharks are called pups. Their
mother swims away. Her job is done.

 She has up to 13 pups at a time.

Bull shark pups are small. They are tasty treats for bigger sharks. The pups must watch out for these hunters. The pups must also hunt for food. They eat fish and other small water animals. Eating prey helps them grow strong. The young bull sharks grow year after year. They are fully grown after 8 to 10 years.

This great white shark hunts smaller fish. It will even eat bull shark pups!

Bull sharks swim through the water unafraid. No other animal hunts them.

 How long do bull sharks live?

# Staying Alive

Adult bull sharks are fierce animals. No other animal hunts them. But they still face dangers. Bull sharks must find enough food to survive. They must also keep their body at a safe temperature. These sharks are **cold-blooded**. Their body temperature matches the temperature of the water.

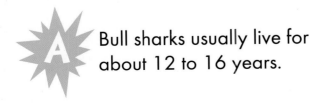 Bull sharks usually live for about 12 to 16 years.

Sometimes the water gets too hot or cold for bull sharks. Then they **migrate** to cooler or warmer waters. Sometimes they travel deep inland up a **freshwater** river. That makes bull sharks unusual. Most sharks can only live in the salty ocean. But bull sharks can live in any kind of water.

A boat floats on the Amazon River in South America. Bull sharks can live in rivers too!

Scientists put a tag on this bull shark. The tag will track where it swims.

# Bull Sharks and People

One of only a few dangers to bull sharks is people. Some people hunt bull sharks. But many bull sharks are caught by mistake. Bull sharks live where many fishers work. The fishers catch fish with large hooks. Sometimes they also catch bull sharks. Now there are fewer bull sharks in the sea.

Bull sharks can be a danger to people, too. The sharks don't hunt people. But they do live where people swim. Sometimes they think a swimmer is prey. Then they attack. But most bull sharks don't harm people. And most people don't want to harm bull sharks. They want bull sharks to stick around for years to come.

 How many people have bull sharks attacked?

**Divers can get close to a shark— if it isn't hungry and doesn't think the diver is an animal.**

 Only 69 attacks have ever been reported. And only 17 of those people died from those attacks.

# Glossary

**anal fin** A fin near a shark's tail.

**cold-blooded** To have the same body temperature as the water or air around itself.

**dorsal fins** Fins on a shark's back that help it keep balance.

**freshwater** Water that is not salty; rivers and lakes are full of fresh water.

**mate** To come together to make babies.

**migrate** To travel a long distance from one place to another.

**pectoral fins** Fins on a fish's sides that help pull it through the water and steer.

**pelvic fins** Fins between the pectoral fins and tail that help a shark keep balance and steer.

**predator** An animal that hunts other animals.

**prey** An animal that is hunted by other animals.

**snout** The nose and mouth of an animal.

# Read More

Dale, Jay. *Deadly and Incredible Animals: Top 10 Marine Animals*. Mankato, Minn.: Smart Apple Media, 2012.

Kennington, Tammy. *Bull Sharks*. Ann Arbor, Mich.: Cherry Lake Pub., 2014.

Pallotta, Jerry. *Hammerhead Vs. Bullshark*. New York: Scholastic, 2011.

# Websites

**Britannica Kids: Bull Shark**
*kids.britannica.com/elementary/art-4721/Bull-shark*

**National Geographic Kids: Bull Sharks**
*kids.nationalgeographic.com/animals/bull-shark/*

**Shark Academy**
*www.oceanicresearch.org/education/shark-academy/shark-academy.html*

# Index

# About the Author

Laura Hamilton Waxman has written and edited many nonfiction books for children. She loves learning about new things—like bull sharks—and sharing what she's learned with her readers. She lives in St. Paul, Minnesota.